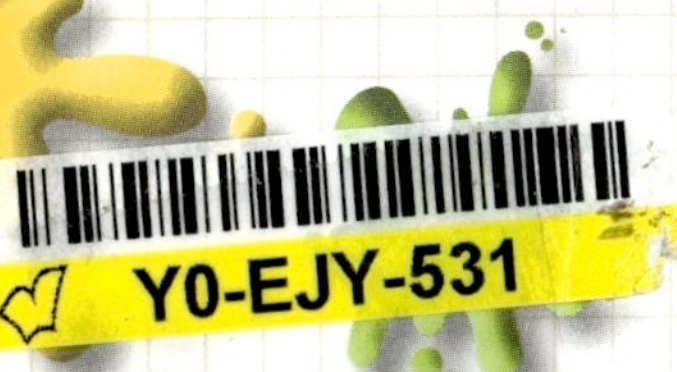

Joke-a-pedia

WARNING:
This book is not suitable for people who lack a sense of humor!

Doctor, Doctor, I think I'm a pack of cookies!

Nonsense, you're just crackers!

Doctor, Doctor, I think I'm a calculator!

That doesn't add up to me!

Doctor, Doctor, I think I'm a baby cod!

Sounds a little fishy to me!

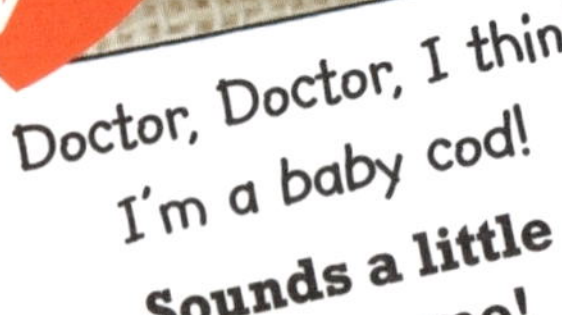

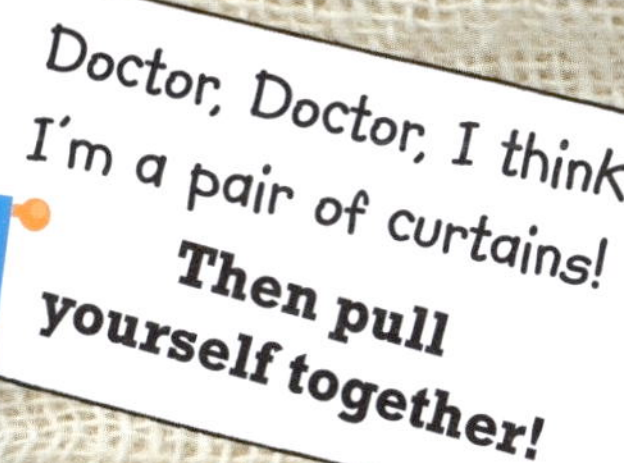

Doctor, Doctor, I think I'm a pair of curtains! **Then pull yourself together!**

Doctor, Doctor, I think I'm a pencil! **I see your point!**

Doctor, Doctor, I think I'm a yo-yo! **How do you feel?** Sometimes I'm up, and sometimes I'm down!

Doctor, Doctor, I think I'm a cat!
Sounds purr-fectly normal to me!
Doctor, Doctor, I think I'm a can of paint!
Put a lid on it!
Doctor, Doctor, I think I'm a fizzy drink!
I find that hard to swallow!

Doctor, Doctor, I think
I'm a cow!

Mooove out of the way!

DOCTOR, DOCTOR

Doctor, Doctor, I think
I'm a submarine!

**You're clearly
out of your depth!**

Doctor, Doctor,
can you help me out?
**Of course, the
door's over there!**

Why did the snake
go to school?

To study hisstory!

What's black and
white and goes
up and down?

A penguin on
a trampoline!

Where do smelly
dinosaurs live?

Jurassic Parp!

Where did the worm
leave its dog?
Tied to a caterPILLAR!

Where do cows go
when it rains?

To the mooovies!

What's a
hedgehog's
favorite snack?
Prickles!

What kind of bugs do
you find in libraries?

Bookworms!

Which dinosaur worked
on construction sites?
Tyrannosaurus wrecks!

Why do cows
make good pianists?
Because they are
so MOO-sical!

Why was the hen banned
from the Internet chat room?
Because her language
was so FOWL!

Where do
polar bears
keep their money?
In snowbanks!

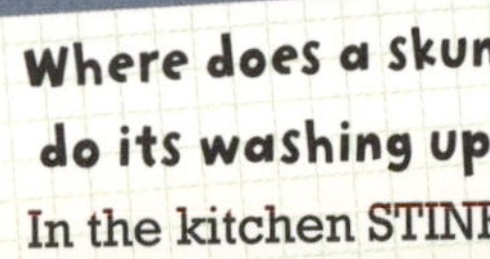

Where does a skunk
do its washing up?
In the kitchen STINK!

What card game
do alligators
play best?
SNAP!

What do
you call a fish
with no eyes?
Fsh!

How did the cow
cause a traffic jam?

It refused to moo-ve from
the middle of the road!

What did the frog order
from the burger joint?
A CROAK and FLIES!

Which side of a bird has the most feathers?

The outside!

Why couldn't the frog drive to work?

Its car was toad away!

Why did the horse take a shower?

Because the cow gave him a pat on the back!

Have you heard about the frog spy?

His name is Pond, James Pond.

How do you stop your dog from barking in the back of your car?

Put it in the front!

What do you call a bee in a bell tower?

A humdinger!

What's a shark's favorite sandwich?

Peanut butter and jellyfish!

Why do cows wear bells?

Because their horns don't work!

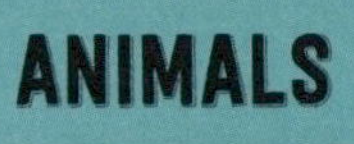

How do you know
when it's been raining
cats and dogs?

The ground is covered
in poodles!

What's a cow's
favorite dance?

The moo-n walk!

Why couldn't
the teddy bear
eat any cake?

Because it was stuffed!

Why can't you order a
clown fish in a restaurant?

Because it tastes funny!

What's the best way to get a fish online?
Catch it Internet!

What part of a tree makes a cat jump?
The bark!

Why was the chick's phone confiscated?
Because he wouldn't stop tweeting!

Why was the sheep sent to its room?
Because it had been baad!

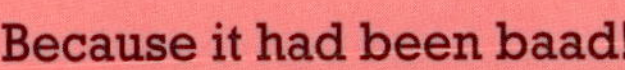

How do bees
style their hair?

With honeycombs!

What do elephants
wear to the beach?

Swimming trunks!

Where do
kittens play?

A-mews-ment parks!

What do you call
a cow eating grass?

A lawn mooer!

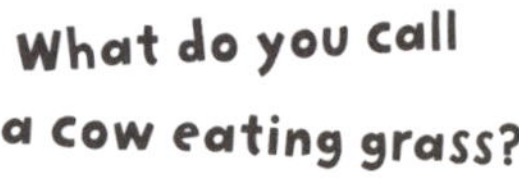

Do cats like green?

Yes, but they
prefer purr-ple!

Why don't grasshoppers cry?
Because they're always hoppy!

If seagulls fly over the sea,
what flies over the bay?

Bay-gulls!

Which animal should you never play games with?

A cheetah!

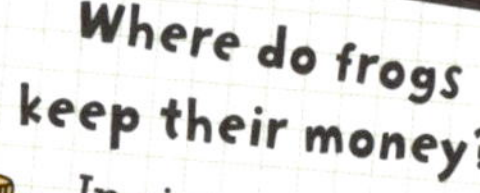

Where do frogs keep their money?

In riverbanks!

How do you stop dogs chasing people on bikes?

Give them skateboards!

When do birds go to hospital?

When they need tweetment!

How do toads
guide their boats
through the mist?

With frog horns!

What do
you call a camel
with three humps?

Humphrey!

What did the spider
say to the fly?

I'm pleased to
eat you!

Why couldn't the pony sing?

Because he was a little HORSE!

ANIMALS

What's black and white and goes up and down?

A zebra in an elevator!

Why don't polar bears wear glasses?

Because they have good ice-sight!

Why did the elephant miss his flight?

He spent too long packing his trunk!

Why do skunks make good judges?

They always bring odor in court!

Why doesn't Tarzan
need a calculator?
Because the jungle
is full of adders!

Why do storks
stand on one leg?

Because they'd fall
over if they lifted both!

Where do city
pigs live?

In styscrapers!

Where do cows
go on vacation?

Moo York City!

KNOCK, KNOCK

KNOCK! KNOCK!
Who's there?
Clare
Clare who?
Clare the room, I'm coming in!
KNOCK! KNOCK!
Who's there?
Ida
Ida who?
Ida hoped you'd know it was me!
KNOCK! KNOCK!
Who's there?
Izzy
Izzy who?
Izzy listening?
KNOCK! KNOCK!
Who's there?
Ken
Ken who?
Ken I come in?

KNOCK! KNOCK!
Who's there?
Luke
Luke who?
Luke out and you'll see!
KNOCK! KNOCK!
Who's there?
Ya
Ya who?
I'm super excited, too!
KNOCK! KNOCK!
Who's there?
Police
Police who?
Police, be quick. It's raining!
KNOCK! KNOCK!
Who's there?
Goat
Goat who?
Goat to the door and open it!

Why did the cookie
go to the hospital?
Because it felt crummy!

Why did the bean
run away from the farm?

**The farmer was
picking on him!**

Why was the
meatball tired?
**Because it was
pasta its bedtime!**

When should you
never suck your food?
Chewsday!

Why did the brainiac
eat her homework?
**Because she thought it
was a piece of cake!**

Why did the Jell-O wobble?
Because he saw the milkshake!

What kind of vegetables
do you find in the gym?
Muscles sprouts!

Have you seen the
new onion website?
Yes, it's a SITE for sore eyes!

What sweet treat
makes lots of mistakes?
D'oh-nuts!

What sound did the grape
make when it got squashed?
A little wine!

What type of ice cream
does Frankenstein eat?
Cookies 'n' scream!

Where do astronauts
keep their sandwiches?
In a launch box!

Did you hear about the angry man who mistook his soap for cheese?

He was foaming at the mouth!

Why did the vegetable house need a new roof?
Because it was full of leeks!

What's the best snack to eat on a roller coaster?
F-RISE and dip!

What's red and hairy and goes up and down?
A raspberry in an elevator!

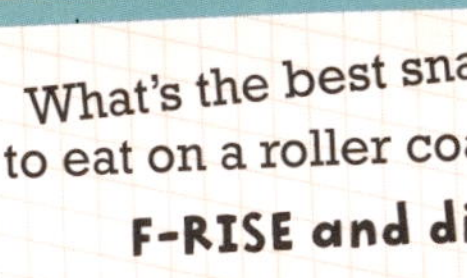
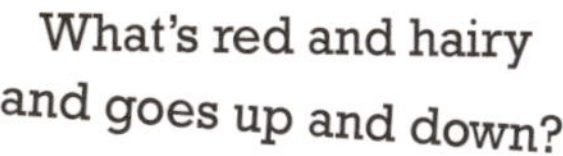

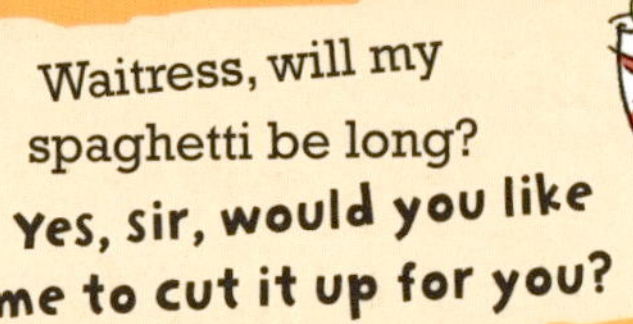

Waitress, will my spaghetti be long?
Yes, sir, would you like me to cut it up for you?

Did you hear about the chef who was crazy about pastries?
She was a dough-nut!

Which snack tastes best on a ghost train?
I scream!

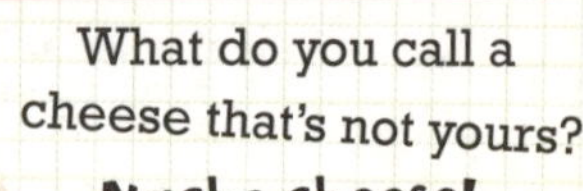

What do you call a cheese that's not yours?
Nacho cheese!

How do you make
a hot dog stand?
Hide its chair!

What's orange and
sounds like a parrot?

A carrot!

Why did the banana
go to hospital?
**Because it wasn't
peeling well!**

Why didn't the knife
trust the spoon?
**Because the spoon
kept stirring things up!**

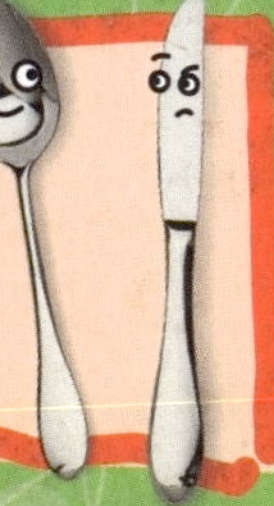

Why didn't anyone eat the overripe banana?
Because it wasn't a-peeling!

Why did the socks sit in the fruit bowl?
They were told they were a pear!

Why did the boy keep his headphones in the fridge?
Because he liked cool music!

Why did the apple run away?
Because the banana split!

Why did the lady
have her hair in a bun?
**Because she'd eaten
all her burgers!**

What do football players eat
at Thanksgiving dinner?
The supper bowl!

Why are basketball
players messy eaters?
**Because they are
always dribbling!**

How do you make
a milkshake?
Tell it a scary story!

RANDOM

Why are noses always
putting their hands up?
Because they love to be picked!

Why did the toilet
see the doctor?
**Because it felt
a little FLUSHED!**

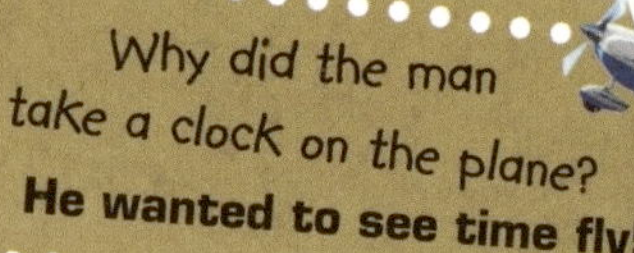

Why did the man
take a clock on the plane?
He wanted to see time fly!

Why did the monster
eat the flashlight?
He wanted a light snack!

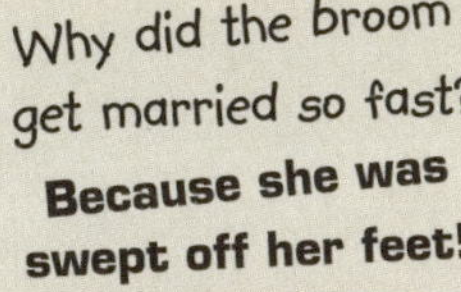

Why did the broom get married so fast?

Because she was swept off her feet!

Why did the elevator visit the doctor?

Because it came down with a cold!

Why did the music-loving boy stick a shoe to his ear?

Because he liked SOUL music!

Why didn't the snowman go to the disco?

Because he had tickets to the snowball!

Why did the computer feel sick?
Because it had too many chips!

Why did the fungus want a bigger house?
He didn't have mushroom!

Why did the teacher wear dark glasses?
Because her students were too bright!

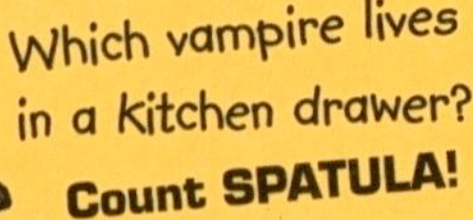

Which vampire lives in a kitchen drawer?
Count SPATULA!

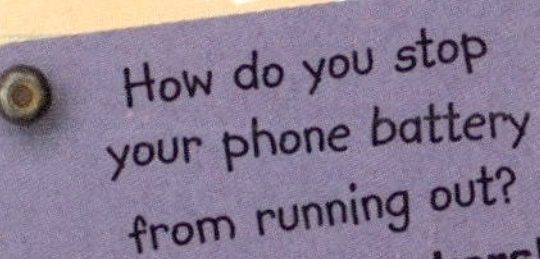

How do you stop
your phone battery
from running out?
Hide its sneakers!

Why did the computer
hide his cheese?
So his mouse wouldn't eat it!

What did the kettle
say when the pan
lost his temper!
Just SIMMER down!

Why did the apartment
building become a library?
**Because it had
so many stories!**

RANDOM

Why did the fool
sit on a clock?
He was told to work overtime!

Why did the fool hang
his phone from the ceiling?
**Because he was told it
was a mobile phone!**

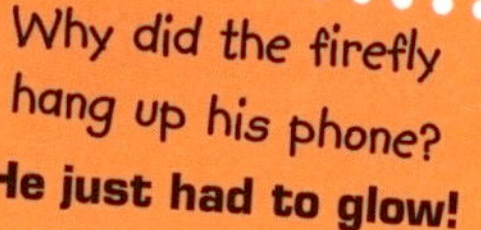

Why did the firefly
hang up his phone?
He just had to glow!

Why did the fool
swallow his laptop?
He thought it was a tablet!

Why did the traffic
light turn red?

**Because the streetlight
saw it changing!**

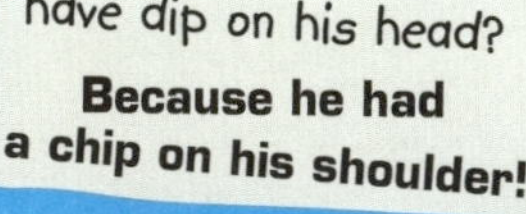

Why did the man
have dip on his head?

**Because he had
a chip on his shoulder!**

Why did the light bulb
fail its exams?

It wasn't very bright!

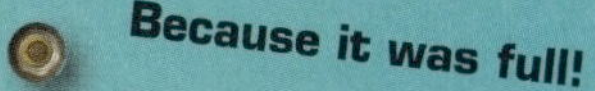

Why did the moon burp?

Because it was full!

Where's the best place to make noise online?
The DIN-ternet!

Why was the shirt sad?
Because the jeans were blue!

How do fishermen catch virtual fish?
Online!

What do elves do after school?
Their gnomework!

What did
the sun say to
the cloud?
You'll be MIST!

Why are scarves
bad at sports?
**Because they prefer
to hang around!**

Which famous
sea creature never
cleans its room?
The Loch MESS Monster!

What did Mr. Volcano say
to Mrs. Volcano when
they got married?
I lava you!

What did the dice say when the cards refused to shuffle?

I'll **DEAL** with you later!

Why are noses with colds super fit?

Because they're always running?

What did the rock star do when he locked himself out?
He sang until he found the right key!

What did the ocean say to the lifeguard?
Nothing, it just waved!

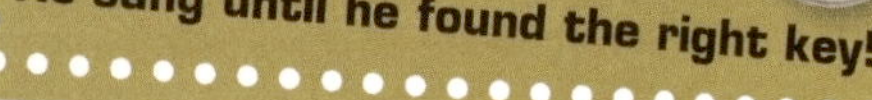

Why was the skeleton feeling lonely?

Because he had **NO BODY** to play with!

What goes HA! HA! BONK!

A man laughing his head off!

What has teeth but cannot eat?

A zipper!

How do you make a toilet roll?

Push it down a hill!

RANDOM

When's the best time
to chop down a tree?
Sep-timber!

What did the curtains
say to the window?
We've got you covered!

How does the sea
wear its hair?

Wavy!

What do sea monsters
eat at parties?
Ships 'n' dip!

What lives at
the bottom of the
sea and shakes?
A nervous wreck!

What's green and refuses
to join in games?
The Incredible Sulk!

Why didn't the artist
leave his bedroom?
**Because he liked
drawing the curtains!**

Did you hear about the plumber
who couldn't mend pipes?
**His business went
down the drain!**

Where does the President of the United States keep his armies?
Up his sleevies!

Why do pirates keep soap in their hats?
To help them wash ashore!

What did the books say when they couldn't agree?
We're just not on the same page!

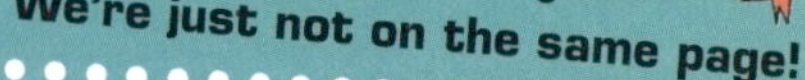

What do you get if you have two running faucets?
A race!

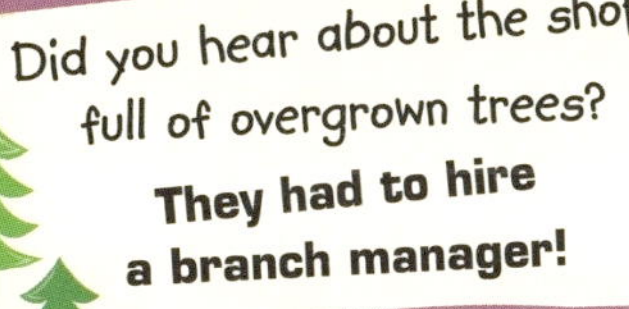

Did you hear about the shop
full of overgrown trees?
**They had to hire
a branch manager!**

Which footwear
will make you jump?
Boo-ts!

What goes up and
down but never moves?
A flight of stairs!

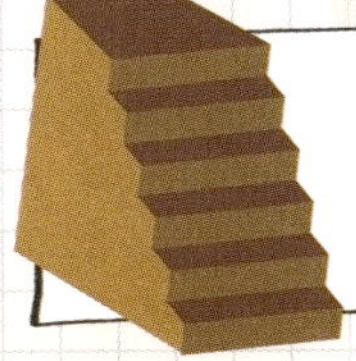

Which worms have spines?
Bookworms!

RANDOM

Why do monsters
eat metal pins?
It's their staple diet!

What's a fisherman's
favorite musical instrument?
The cast-a-nets!

How do snowmen
get to work?
On bICICLES!

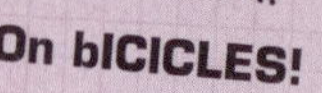

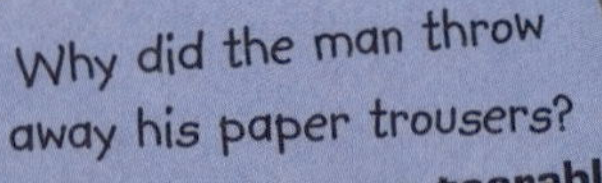

Why did the man throw
away his paper trousers?
Because they were tearable!

Why couldn't the doctor see her patients?

Because she'd lost her glasses!

Why are hairdressers never late for work?

Because they know all the shortcuts!

What do you call a man with a car on his head?

Jack!

When is the best time to visit the dentist?

Tooth hurty!

THE BEST JOKE I EVER HEARD...